What's Wrong? 🔍

IN DINOSAUR TIMES

Catherine Veitch

Illustrated by **Fermin Solis**

Quarto is the authority on a wide range of topics.

Quarto educates, entertains and enriches the lives of our readers—enthusiasts and lovers of hands-on living.

www.quartoknows.com

Author: Catherine Veitch
Illustrator: Fermin Solis
Designer: Victoria Kimonidou
Editor: Emily Pither

© 2019 Quarto Publishing plc

First Published in 2019 by QEB Publishing,
an imprint of The Quarto Group.
6 Orchard Road
Suite 100
Lake Forest, CA 92630
T: +1 949 380 7510
F: +1 949 380 7575
www.QuartoKnows.com

A CIP record for this book is available from the Library of Congress.

ISBN 978-1-78603-477-9

Manufactured in Shenzhen, China HH112018

9 8 7 6 5 4 3 2 1

MIX
Paper from
responsible sources
FSC® C017606
FSC
www.fsc.org

PSST!
Dinosaurs lived a LONG time ago. When you see MYA next to a date, this means **million years ago**.

WHAT'S WRONG IN DINOSAUR TIMES?

Hi, we're Leah and Eddie! Join us as we travel back in time and discover all sorts of interesting creatures in dinosaur times.

But watch out! In each scene there are **five** out-of-place things. Can you find them all? Look carefully, as some are hard to spot.

Turn to the back of the book for handy explanations about what's wrong, as well as a **strange but true!** fact per scene—these might seem wrong, but they're actually right!

LET THE SEARCH BEGIN!

CONTENTS

EARLY DINOSAURS

LATE TRIASSIC (237-201 MYA)

The Earth was a scorching hot, dry desert when dinosaurs first appeared on it. Can you spot **five things** that are wrong or don't belong here? Can you say what's wrong with them? There are **two clues** to help you.

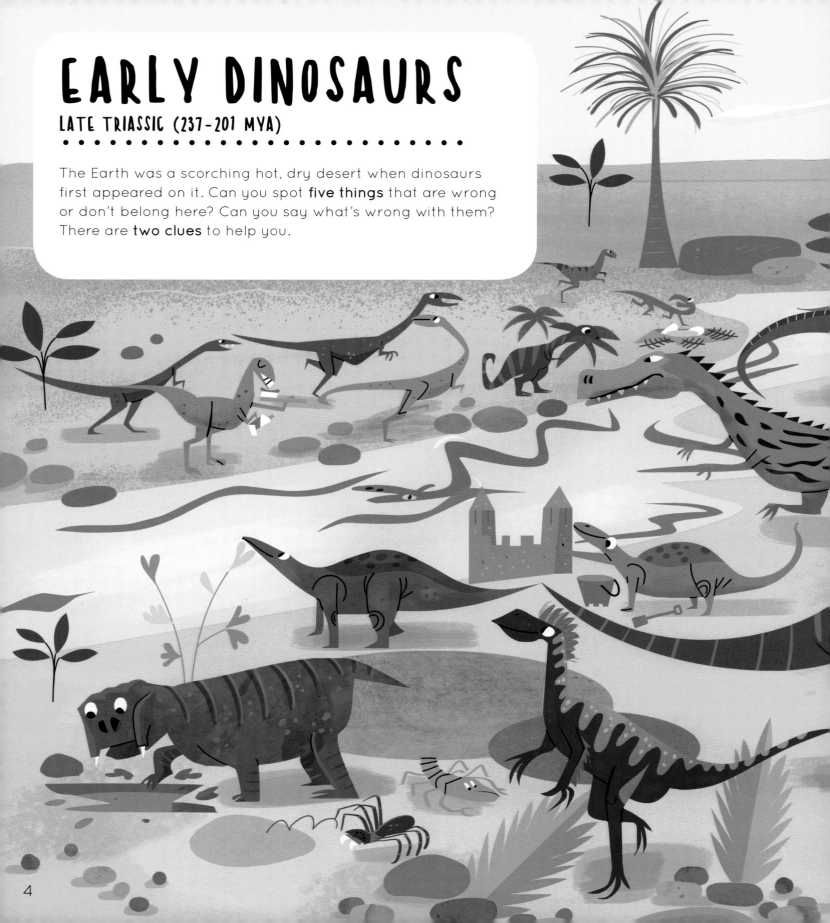

5

FIERY PLANET
EARLY TO MID JURASSIC (201-164 MYA)

The land changed a lot in dinosaur times as fiery volcanoes blasted out scalding ash, gas, and rocks over it. Run for cover! Can you spot **five things** that are wrong or don't belong here? Can you say what's wrong with them? There are **two clues** to help you.

EARTHSHAKERS

LATE JURASSIC (164-145 MYA)

These dinosaurs are huge! Many of them are plant-eaters, but watch out for the meat-eaters! See if you can spot **five things** that are wrong or don't belong here. Can you say what's wrong with them? There are **two clues** to help you.

9

DINO DINNERS
EARLY CRETACEOUS (145-101 MYA)

Time for lunch! Many grazing dinosaurs munched on moss and ferns. Yuck! Can you spot **five things** that are wrong or don't belong here? Can you say what's wrong with them? There are **two clues** to help you.

WATERY WORLD
EARLY CRETACEOUS (145-101 MYA)

Much of the land had flooded by the Early Cretaceous period and many dinosaurs feasted on fish in the huge rivers. See if you can spot **five things** that are wrong or don't belong here. Can you say what's wrong with them? There are **two clues** to help you.

13

NIFTY NESTERS
LATE CRETACEOUS (101-66 MYA)

This is a noisy, crazy crèche! Lots of dinosaur eggs were eaten by other hungry dinosaurs, so they had lots of babies in the hope that some might survive. Can you spot **five things** that are wrong or don't belong here? Can you say what's wrong with them? There are **two clues** to help you.

DINO BATTLES

LATE CRETACEOUS (101-66 MYA)

In the Late Cretaceous period, plant-eating dinosaurs had horns, spikes and frills to protect them from the sharp teeth and claws of fierce, meat-eating dinosaurs. There were some mighty battles! Can you spot **five things** that are wrong or don't belong here? Can you say what's wrong with them? There are **two clues** to help you.

BEASTS OF THE DEEP
TRIASSIC-CRETACEOUS (237-66 MYA)

Dinosaurs may have ruled on land, but there were also some huge, weird and scary reptiles in the sea. Dive down deep and take a look. Can you spot **five things** that are wrong or don't belong here? Can you say what's wrong with them? There are **two clues** to help you.

MONSTERS IN THE SKIES

TRIASSIC-CRETACEOUS (237- 66 MYA)

There were no planes back in dinosaur times, but the skies were full of massive, mean-looking, flying reptiles. Can you spot **five things** that are wrong or don't belong here? Can you say what's wrong with them? There are **two clues** to help you.

EARLY DINOSAURS

(1) *Guaibasaurus* may have had a head crest but scientists don't think it was rainbow colored!

(2) *Coelophysis* could run very fast to catch insects and small reptiles for their dinner, but they didn't dress up in running gear!

(3) The meat-eating *Eoraptor* had lots of small, razor-sharp teeth to tear into its prey, but toothbrushes weren't around in dinosaur times.

(4) There were no flowering plants in the Triassic period, and there were certainly no flower pots!

(5) Dinosaurs didn't build sandcastles! Although, some dinosaurs may have buried their eggs in sandy soil.

⭐ **Strange but true!** *Lystrosaurus* was one of a few mammals who lived at this time and could burrow underground to escape predators and danger.

These **five things** are wrong in the picture:

FIERY PLANET

(1) The dinosaur times were noisy, with roaring beasts, blasting volcanoes, and ear-splitting earthquakes, but headphones weren't around then.

(2) *Omeisaurus* had a very long neck but it didn't get tied up in knots!

(3) Of course dinosaurs didn't wear pajamas, or any clothes!

(4) Dinosaurs didn't play tennis, as tennis wasn't invented until 1873.

(5) Dinosaurs that walked on two legs could run faster than those that walked on four legs, but no dinosaur would have traveled on skis.

⭐ **Strange but true!** *Omeisaurus* had a neck which was four times longer than its body.

These **five things** are wrong in the picture:

EARTHSHAKERS

(1) Umbrellas didn't exist in dinosaur times, but dinosaurs wouldn't have needed them as rain slipped off their scaly skin.

(2) Dinosaurs didn't wear armor. But some, such as *Stegosaurus*, had spikes, horns, and frills on their bodies that protected them like armor.

(3) Of course dinosaurs didn't wear rain boots, as these weren't around then.

(4) Giraffes are alive today and didn't exist in dinosaur times.

(5) *Stegosaurus* didn't have bows on its back. It had enormous, diamond-shaped plates along its spine.

⭐ **Strange but true!** This may look like a dinosaur wearing a hat, but it's actually a *Giraffatitan*—a dinosaur with a tall, arched skull.

These **five things** are wrong in the picture:

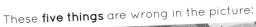

DINO DINNERS

1. Dinosaurs weren't bookworms, as books hadn't been invented back then and dinosaurs couldn't read!

2. *Deinonychus* didn't eat ice cream! They were ferocious hunters, chasing and attacking their prey in packs.

3. Of course bicycles weren't around in dinosaur times, and many dinosaurs would be too big to fit on bikes!

4. There were no dogs in dinosaur times.

5. There were no hats or sunglasses in dinosaur times. But there were plenty of huge, leafy forests to give shade from the sun.

★ **Strange but true!** *Nigersaurus's* mouth was the widest part of its head. It was like a living lawnmower, gulping down mouthfuls of plants from the ground.

These **five things** are wrong in the picture:

WATERY WORLD

These **five things** are wrong in the picture:

1. Dinosaurs didn't use fishing rods, as they weren't invented then.

2. There weren't any bridges in dinosaur times.

3. Chickens are alive today and weren't around back then. But some small dinosaurs did look a bit like chickens!

4. Of course dinosaurs didn't swim with inflatable rings.

5. The oldest soccer ball found was made almost 500 years ago, but they weren't around in dinosaur times.

★ **Strange but true!** *Baryonyx* had a huge 14-inch (35-cm) claw on each thumb. It was thought it used its claws to spear fish for lunch. Gulp!

NIFTY NESTERS

1. Dinosaurs didn't dress up in burglar outfits, but some dinosaurs such as this *Bambiraptor* stole eggs to eat.

2. This spiky *Edmontonia* is in the wrong nest!

3. Dinosaurs didn't play instruments to hush their babies to sleep.

4. Baby dinosaurs didn't sleep in cots! Many slept with up to 25 of their siblings in giant nests, which were huge hollows in the ground.

5. Strollers were not invented in dinosaur times. Many reptiles left their eggs after laying them so they would not have carried their young like this.

★ **Strange but true!** This may look like a purple duck or chicken, but it's actually the *Bambiraptor*—a small, fast dinosaur which ran on 2 legs.

These **five things** are wrong in the picture:

DINO BATTLES

1. Dinosaurs didn't have roller skates!

2. *Gallimimus* couldn't do kung-fu like this, but it could swivel its head all the way around, which was a cool party trick!

3. Dinosaurs didn't wear boxing gloves. Small dinosaurs zipped around fast and got away quickly, rather than hanging around to fight.

4. This huge *Anatotitan* is heading for a fall, as it's too hefty to climb a tree!

5. Trophies don't grow on trees!

★ **Strange but true!** *Parasaurolophus* communicated by pushing air through a hollow bone at the top of its head to make a tooting sound.

These **five things** are wrong in the picture:

BEASTS OF THE DEEP

1. *Elasmosaurus* didn't need diving gear to swim! They could breathe underwater and used their flippers to push themselves through the water.

2. A shipwreck doesn't belong here! There were no ships in dinosaur times.

3. This mermaid shouldn't be here—mermaids are figures from myths and legends.

4. Penguins are alive today and weren't around back then.

5. Dinosaurs didn't wear swimming trunks, or any clothes for that matter!

★ **Strange but true!** This beady-eyed *Opthalmosaurus* really had eyes as big as dinner plates! It could see and hunt its prey hundreds of yards deep, where the ocean was darkest.

These **five things** are wrong in the picture:

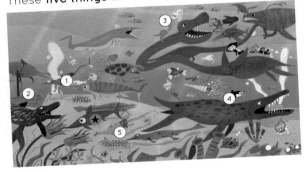

MONSTERS IN THE SKIES

1. Ducks are alive today and weren't around back then. Although, some flying reptiles looked a bit like ducks.

2. These delicate wings belong to a butterfly, not a big flying reptile!

3. This hefty *Triceratops* is too heavy to fly. And it would need a huge parachute to carry its weight in the air!

4. Of course, there were no balloons in dinosaur times!

5. Flying reptiles didn't own fishing nets, but many, such as *Pterodaustro*, used their big beaks as nets to scoop up fish.

★ **Strange but true!** *Quetzalcoatlus* was the largest flying creature. Standing, it was as big as a giraffe, and scientists believe it used its wings to walk.

These **five things** are wrong in the picture: